DO THE WALLS

Do the Walls Come Down?

Meditations of a Lifer

Chris Lambrianou

Hodder & Stoughton
LONDON SYDNEY AUCKLAND

British Library Cataloguing in Publication Data
A record for this title is available from the British Library

ISBN 0 340 67119 X

Typeset by Palimpsest Book Production Limited,
Polmont, Stirlingshire
Printed and bound in Great Britain by
Cox & Wyman Ltd, Reading, Berks.

Hodder and Stoughton Ltd
A division of Hodder Headline PLC
338 Euston Road
London NW1 3BH

For

My children, my friends – all lovely people who have blessed and enriched my life.

My father the Marathon Man who ran with strength down the years. R.I.P.

St Aldate's and the Rector, David MacInnes, for continuous support and direction.

Freddy Sanson who was a good pal.
(Died in Hull Jail. R.I.P.)

Joyce Martin for being my friend and for typing all the papers I put before her. Thanks Stan!

Jessica and the girls at Downy House. Bless you all from the child in me.

Jim Anderson

Father Alex

and Mike Kendrick who was okay!

And finally to Pat Dinneen and Jenny Upton – two angels!

With tears of blood he cleansed the hand,
the hand that held the steel.
For only blood can wipe out blood
and only tears can heal.
And the crimson stain that was of Cain
became Christ's snow-white seal.

From *The Ballad of Reading Gaol*
by Oscar Wilde

What lies behind us and before us are small matters,
compared to what lies within us.

Ralph Waldo Emerson

Contents

Foreword

When I heard about the Prison Fellowship back in 1978 I was excited because I knew that, indirectly, it changed people's lives; more directly, it was Jesus Christ himself. If He could change my life He was able to change even the most hardened of criminals. It did not seem strange to me therefore to be driving to Coldingley Prison with Chris's father in order for him to visit his son. Although I had heard from Chris I had not met him until that moment, and it was moving for me to see these two grown men embrace. I was not made to feel awkward as we sat down at one of the many tables set out for visiting time. A few months later Chris's father died. I know this was a very difficult time for Chris as there were so many things he had not been able to convey to his father.

Through the prison chaplain I was invited to join in the Sunday Service. It meant going through more security doors and passing by the garden that Chris had told me about and which he had been able to plant and care for. I took part in the worship several times in both chapels. It was there that I met members who came regularly from the Prison Fellowship to encourage the congregation. Out of that time grew a small prayer group.

I was in no doubt that Chris wanted to start a new life since his conversion in 1975. He longed for his own family with positive relationships – something not easily understood within an institution. Love and compassion seem more a figment of the imagination in such places, but Chris craved for them. When he was given his freedom in 1983 I kept in close touch with him. During this time he met Caroline, they were married and soon after, he became the father of twins. I was asked to be godmother to both Holly and Christopher, which made me feel both happy and a little apprehensive. I had to remind myself that I had come to trust in the same Saviour as Chris and Caroline had, but life for them I later realised, was not going to be easy. The Prison Fellowship know how vital it is to train for marriage: something we all need, but how much more for those who have not experienced family life for themselves. Chris and Caroline wanted their marriage to work, and they had three more children to love and care for. Sadly it was not to last; but his children will remain a constant source of joy to Chris.

Chris has always wanted to provide for his family, so he took what work he could find. I remember visiting him at the Lazarus Tip, a place where he could enjoy solitude. He is currently working the The Ley Community near Oxford. This is a rehabilitation centre for drug and alcohol offenders. He has encouraged them, through his own experiences, to start new relationships and lead new lives, knowing that as he was taken out of the pit of despair others can do the same.

Chris is full of hope, he acknowledges his own weaknesses and he puts his trust in the living Lord Jesus. For him the walls have come tumbling down. Society must stop judging and recognise that it is possible to change; we all have the freedom to choose – Chris has chosen the better path, a new life in Christ Jesus.

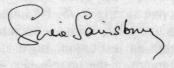

July 1996

If you would life to find out more about Prison Fellowship please contact: PO Box 945, Chelmsford, Essex CM2 7RD (Tel: 01245 490249).

The Walls Come Down

One night as I was praying I distinctly heard a voice say, 'Chris, don't speak these prayers. Write them down.' I felt annoyed because I didn't want to lose that great feeling of God's love which one can only feel in deep contemplation. Nevertheless I did obey and sat looking out into the darkness of night. I wrote down my prayers not knowing from one day to the next where they would lead me. Each day gave up a reflection to be perused.

About fifteen days into my meditations the unthinkable happened. The one thing I had dreaded, the one thing I wasn't prepared to give up was slipping from my grasp. Like Abraham I was being asked to give up my Isaac, the person I loved most. My father became ill and was taken into hospital. He was diagnosed as having terminal cancer. Only a few weeks previously, he had come to visit me with Susie, a wonderful friend. He appeared quite fit and well, but now as I looked down at him in a hospital bed he was a very frail, sick old man. The strength he had so often given to me was now gone and the light in his tired eyes was becoming extinct. God bless him. This was my test. Could I give him up to God's love?

I can remember when I let go. I went out into the prison garden where I worked and saw a beautiful red rose with a single raindrop on one of its petals. It looked like a perfect tear, almost pearl-like, yet crystal clear. I looked up at the trees and saw the wind rustling among the leaves. My eyes saw the vastness of the sky and I thought, 'Death, where is thy sting? Where, grave, thy victory?' My father was more with me in death than he had ever been in life. Now I could see him in all the facets of my life. All the walls and fences had indeed come down and all that was left was love.

1

Jesus, When?

I didn't expect prison to have a heart so I never looked for one. I didn't expect prison to change me for it has never changed anyone for the better. Harsh regimes, hard beds, cold walls, bitter voices, banging doors, jingling keys, bread and water, and segregation are not conducive to inner peace. In the prisoner's head are the noises of his environment and a continuous internal dialogue. Keeping sane is a daily exercise carried out within the brain.

Reality used to be a friend of mine, but prisoners are the ones who walk in the world of the paranoid, bankrupt, beat-up; filled with hurt and envy for what the others have on the other side of the wall. Emptiness is the night-time filled with stillness and regrets; souls in search of something to hang on to, but there is nothing. Sex comes out of the comic caricatures, the concept of a woman leaps from the pages of the latest pornographic magazine going the rounds, like a well-worn prostitute, folded and dirtied, crumpled and mean, used and abused, finally cut up and put on a wall. God, if you're out there listening, show me a bridge out of this madness.

Day by Day

Don't let anyone tell you crime pays. Banged away, inside the cell, whispers and rumours float on the air. A man has just bought it on 'D' wing.

A cold blade rams home its hard, internal, fatal wound. He's dead. Why? For a small transistor radio or half an ounce of tobacco. Screams come from another young kid getting raped and abused; the abused become abusers.

> Walls within, and walls without,
> and you wonder why I shout,
> 'Get me out! Just get me out!'

To my knees I sink, but then I don't believe anyway, I don't believe in me. So if you're out there listening, help me. I am drowning in my sea of doubt. I don't want Eden. I don't even care about getting out. Just take away my blindfold and let me see you, the wonder of love's golden fields, the touch of the sun, the silence of the wind as it caresses my cheeks. Let me smell perfume on the breeze, let my eyes release the pain in my soul so that I may swim in your love. If you are really Lord of Lords, give my soul back to me. Father, you made me. You have an investment in my life, so take everything the devil didn't want and set me free from this web of lies. Let me live from day to day and, for today, just let me be really me.

Part of You

I yearn to find a decent woman, a mother for my children,
　　a woman to share my trials and joys,
to share the joy of knowing you, almighty Father of all
　　creation, to build a future which brings credit to both
　　you and my earthly father.

I yearn to work with peace in my heart,
to work for a just wage for my labours, and to give my
　　all for those who you choose to be my family.

I yearn for justice,
I believe in all that is good and decent and fine in
　　human nature.

I yearn to work for you and with you.

I yearn to know true friends, who want to be my friends,
　　and who appreciate whatever good qualities they
　　may feel I have to offer.

The silence of my heart tells me that I will, one day, be
　　the man you always wanted me to be,
and that I can and will be a true friend.

I yearn to hear children's laughter, to smile with a
　　full heart,
to walk where there are no bars, no bolts, no walls, no
　　wires, no locks.

I yearn for a place where a man can hold out his arms in
　　a fullness of heart to his loved ones, and receive a

response of oneness that transcends earthly pleasures and joys.

Lord, to walk as far as the eye can see, and look up into the vastness of the night sky and to know that I am part of you and that you are part of me.

Forgive Them

Prison, what you do to people is truly indescribable, for you truly do fill lives with anger and hatred, bitterness and frustration!

Why do you feed on such squalor? You are not and never were the answer, but still you persist and exist.

All I have to combat you with is one who knew you well, and was truly troubled by your walls. His wisdom tried to breach those walls and oftentimes succeeded, as it still does today.

But you in your knowing ignorance keep pushing him away as a fool, because your knowledge of good has become faded.

So, I wait in my room for the ascending silence which brings the deep peace I require to restore my heart and soul and retain my sense of balance and sanity.

Father, our Lord said, 'Forgive them, for they know not what they do.' I would like to endorse that very fact. They still do not know! And that is extremely sad.

Prison Problems

Prison problems and problem prisons. How does one just walk away from it all?

It leaves me with a feeling of being covered in rank filth. The stench of it fills my nostrils. The slime of it pulls and saps at my inner strength.

Lord, I really need this quiet time after nine at night to renew my inner resources in silent communion with you.

The advice, the questions, the 'have you heards', the 'do you knows', the food, the 'I don't cares', the 'I hate the world', 'I hate people', 'I hate screws', 'I hate life', the divided lives. I want to put up my hands, Lord, and say, 'Have you heard of my Saviour, Jesus Christ?'

But I don't have to do that, because I make no secret of the fact that I believe in you, and everybody knows, anyway.

So, I just put my fingers in my ears, mentally, and try not to let it affect me. But it does affect me, whether I want it to or not, and it's extremely hard to shut it out.

Reality

To a woman with three children whose husband has deserted her, reality is a broken marriage, loneliness, her children crying, sleepless nights, despair and pain.

Reality is a man, old and grey, sleeping rough and then at daybreak – tottering off on his road to nowhere, his only possession a battered violin.

Reality is the man at the entrance to a tube station, begging pennies as he plays 'Jesu, joy of man's desiring' to the hordes of rushing commuters.

Reality, Lord, is a father visiting his son in prison, heartbroken at his son's folly, giving him comfort, solace, warmth and a smile. Reality is when the father cannot make it any more – and the son's grief at the loss of contact, and the shame of knowing that the old man loves him – but can never respect him.

Reality is a priest, still trying to tell a family who have lost a loved one that they can find a God who loves them.

Father, reality is your son dying on the cross, showing us that life is full of pain, distress, sorrow and an uphill climb, with little support or comfort. And reality is proof that the hill can be climbed.

To Be Whole

When I am in trouble I say my prayers but my soul
    demands more.
It demands that I thank you for answering my prayers.
Perhaps I will go to church – another concession to
    God?

I sit in church, silently and reverently but nothing really
    happens
and my only source of contentment is that I know you
    want me here.
Why? I don't know!

It's not long before you throw me to my knees.
More and more I feel like a man running in a race who has
    trained for the distance but finds he has to discharge
    so much useless baggage to last the pace.

You have changed me, and so has prison.
What is prison? Pain, sin, deceit, humiliation, degrada-
    tion, falseness, lies, mistrust, suspicion, ridicule –
All these things and more.
It's society's dustbin.

Lord, I want to be a whole man, not one person on the
    inside and another on the outside, both striving.

The one on the inside is alive, alert, loving, caring, com-
    passionate, communing with you, Lord, in prayer
    and contemplation.
The other on the outside is blind, hurt, sad, wretched,

alone, ruined, having to live a lie to make satisfaction
   for a crime which he did not commit,
and belonging to a group of people he hardly knows
having travelled through every hell-hole in the English
   penal system.

Yes, sometimes it pains me, Lord! Sometimes it hurts.
So forgive me if at times I get a little angry,
and let me try a little harder to see the good.
It's there, Lord,
Underneath the dross.

Father, if I have done any good thing today, please
   accept it,
and let it be put in my deposit box, which is in your
   vault.

Poverty

This word – poverty – just what does it mean?

To have no friends, no family, no love.
No hope, no courage, no faith, no God?

There was a time when to have no money would have
    been poverty,
but to be a man with no friends, is surely to be the poorest
    of the poor,
and to be a man with no family is almost unthinkable.
A man without love in his life would be a man of extreme
    emptiness:

A man with no hope!

What could he possibly see, feel or touch?

A man without courage, he would be very poor indeed,
    with no confidence to face life, to face people or
    himself.
He would be perhaps the saddest of all the poverty-
    stricken.
But the man with no faith – where would he be?

Where would he fit in?

To believe in nothing and no one, not even himself, or
    the ground under his feet,
or the promise of tomorrow, to have no future.

Such a man would bring tears to your eyes.

Oh Lord, I believe you would pity such a man.
The man who has no God –
he is the poorest of us all.

Not to be able to hear the sublime wonder of your love
    in a piece of music,
Not to see your face beaming down, as the sun casts forth
    its radiant rays of goodness.
Not to be able to look around and see the trees, shrubs
    and plants bursting forth into blossom, to see the
    richness of the earth and nature abounding with so
    many good things.
Not to acknowledge that you – the true God – are
    everywhere and in everything.

Today, and always,
I do feel a deeper reverence, pride and respect in the
    knowledge that the God who does all this is indeed
    my Father.

Special Crosses

I wonder how you felt upon the cross at Calvary –

Let down? Hurt? Neglected? Unforgiving?
No!
If I recall your words, I believe you said, 'Father, forgive
    them for they know not what they do.'
Forgive.

Forgive is such a pretty word,
but very few people really know what it means and
    moreover a lot of people
don't really want to be forgiven.
But, regardless, you forgive the greatest pain, the greatest
    rejection, humiliation, degradation.

They made a mockery of you, the few things which you
    possessed they sold for money to buy a jug of wine
    and a woman for comfort.
My God, the Son of God, they sold for comfort!

And you say, 'Father, forgive them for they know not
    what they do!'

I see through your eyes that they did not know.

So, I too ask not only for my own forgiveness but for
    their forgiveness.
And that more and more will come to know the forgive-
    ness which I speak of,
then they can come to know you as I know you.

As for friends, Lord, I recall your friends were few. Simon
Peter denied you. How many more lived in fear and
trembling, afraid to acknowledge you as a friend?
Yet, secretly in their denial of you, they could not have
seen they were denying themselves.

As only you can help us bear our special crosses, give us
your fortitude as we walk our path,
until the day we reach our true place in heaven with
you.

Sin

Sin is the evil which makes me judge my brother and my sister and find them both wanting. Sin is the 'shifty-eyed' look of suspicion which makes me cynical and bitter. Sin is the pride that makes me reject the good in other people and strike out in anger.

Sin is what makes a person stand in your house, Father, and deem themselves better than another. Sin is the evil I do and the good that I don't do. Sin is being unable to trust you, Father, and putting trust in man or woman instead.

Sin is in loving people but not letting you love them through me. Sin is thinking I can make it on my own without your help. Sin is the reason I have to come trembling to you.

Sin is war, hunger, disease and every kind of misery. Sin is discrimination against people based on sex, race, colour, language or religion. Sin is the selfishness which stops me from helping or sharing.

Sin is the cross we bear. Sin, Father, brings me to my knees in supplication, and like the prodigal son I say: 'Lord, I am not worthy to sit at your table.'

Lord, deal with me as you will from now on. I have nothing. I am nothing.

Accept me, pitiful and small sinful man that I am. Father, I flinch from nothing, and accept your will for me as a human being. Without you there is nothing to go forward for.

Accept Me

I ask you to accept my gifts:
my good points and my bad.
Accept my weakness,
my fear of living without pride or self-respect.
Accept me as you made me, perfectly.

Father, my pride has had to change with the changing
   times.
What was, once, so important to me is so unimportant
   now.
What can man offer me? Nothing compared with the
   breath in my body.
Can he give me the friendship – that you give me?
Can he make me see the truth – as you do?
Guide, me, Lord, to the totality of my true self.
Give me the strength to do your will.
Take the pride which says 'No'.
Take the bitterness.
Take the anger I feel for my brother,
which will not leave me in peace.
Help me to forgive a world which will not forgive me.
Father, lift me above myself.

The Gift of Awareness

Try as I may I can never care for you as much as you
    care for me.
No man can ever have the ability to care as you care,
to love as you love,
to feel as you feel,
to give as you give,
to reach out as you reach out,
to touch people as you touch them.

In many ways, Lord, you too are serving a long sentence
    and we are the human bars.
How you must cry for your human race.
If only they would cry for you.

Every nation, every denomination could be joined together
    in one, its heart open to you.

Lord of creation, teach us to care. Grant us the gift of
    awareness.

Friendship

Sometimes, Lord, because people don't live up to our expectations, we feel hurt, neglected and defeated. Grant us the ability to try to live up to our own expectations, and, if we fall down, grant our friends the ability to put up with our failings and bear with us, so that we may truly learn to be a friend.

Father, let me not make too many demands on others, but let me indeed strive to make the right demands of myself. I would really and truly like to smile and laugh from the heart. After all, it has been such a long time, as you know. It would do me a power of good, that's the plain truth!

To have friend, you have to be a friend. Perhaps we all fall short and need someone to teach us how not to be just a friend on the human relationship level, but how even more so on a greater scale a responsible friend of this earth, our world. To be a friend of mankind, which is something far finer and bigger than we can imagine.

Lord Jesus, you were such a friend and, moreover, the kind of example of which I speak.

Time

Because I live in prison, time has great meaning for me and the word *time* has a way of being very profound.

Perhaps this is because we all have a tendency to look at time, or rather to watch it.

We say we never have enough of it, not even time to stop and think about the effect it has on us as human beings.

Somehow, Father, you must see all this from your watchtower and for our own good – slow us down to your pace.

I believe you do this in many ways, through sickness, bereavement, poverty, both spiritual and moral, financial and physical.

Man is truly a foolish creature in your sight, the time he wastes. Yet you still love him.

My time with you is a kind of remission.
Where you are, there are no walls, wires or bars
and I can see the sky –
I see a bird on the wing,
and the giant man-made silver birds with the sun shining
    on their wings.

Lord, in humility my heart sings to your heart in silent wonder.

Accept, Lord

Father, if any act of kindness on my part is misconstrued, please forgive me, for I am truly sorry. I only want to rest easy in the knowledge that I have made you smile and that all the good I do goes back to you. For without you I would have nothing at all to give. I say this in all sincerity.

If it be your will to give me any good thing, please also give me the ability to share it with others.

I thank you for the gift of today. I found an oak tree. I might also have found some good friends, if it be your will.

Today I was also able to plant some flowers. I would appreciate it if you would breathe life into them, so that they might give pleasure to all the people who pass by them and, if possible, would you give us a little sunshine to warm our bones.

Tonight I ask specially in my prayers for your blessing for Hugh, our chaplain, and also for the students who are trying to better their lives.

I pray for prisoners and their families. I pray for our keepers and their families. May you bless all with peace, health and happiness.

Lord, accept tonight for all its doubts, trials and tribulations and lead me into a new day filled with trust and hope in the mercy of your love.

Help Me

Perhaps if I was in a situation where I could walk away and forget, then true forgiveness would be possible. But when I am confronted daily by one who has committed an act of evil against me, or the things which I hold dear, then I am in extreme distress. But when I imagine our Lord saying 'hate the sin but love the sinner', I have to believe that he is telling me that human nature in itself is basically very good. But there is in this world a spirit of evil which invades a man's very soul, if he does not stand guard over it with his very life.

Where is the man who is brave enough to brush evil aside with the contempt it deserves and therefore bring peace and light into any situation which it has touched?

Lord, make me such a person in your name, because of my own will and strength it would not be possible.

Lord, I Believe

Lord, I believe you answer all the prayers as you see fit; not as I will but as you will.

Father, when I pray my words are silent and it is only in the silence that I can reach you. It is the key to all secrets, this silence.

When all external and internal noises are cast aside, when the voices of doubt, fear and anxiety are all stilled, then in the silence of the void, in communion with you, I ask you to fill me with your peace and love. And let me see the world through your eyes, the eyes of your love.

Your silence touches my silence and I know that you are you, as you have always been and always will be.

Father, I am finding it very difficult to speak the words of my heart and so the things I wish to say just won't come out.

How does one pray?

My God, are words ever enough?

Words are clever and have a subtle way of shaking off the rare beauty of simplicity.

I pray, Father, that you will help me rid myself of the artfulness and subtlety of words and help me to get back my spiritual simplicity, so that I can say 'be merciful to me, a sinner', and mean it in your sight. May I truly forgive and not seek for the forgiveness of man, but await your forgiveness which transcends all forgiveness and needs no words.

Broken Wings

Did my mother know that she was going to die?
If so, she kept the knowledge to herself
and bore it all with great strength and dignity.
It is only now, after many years, that I can talk about her
    death with some degree of freedom.

At the time, I had no faith, but the strange thing was that
    I turned against you. I hurled profanities at your
    very name.

I still recall picking a flower from one of the wreaths at
    her funeral and throwing it into the open mouth of
    the grave.
That tiny flower represented my spirit going down into
    the darkness.

Lord, truly I couldn't understand why.

Lord, Father, do we understand joy as you understand
    it?
The release of my mother's spirit from that pain.
The perfect peace, the joy of her spirit, to be again with
    you, Lord.

I praise your name for taking all your children with broken
    wings and giving them greater things.

Freedom

There is a breeze which blows into each man's life,
when he truly knows for certain what freedom really is,
when he knows that only in you can be found real
    rock-hard reality and freedom to be himself.

This, my God, my friend, is what I truly desire
And maybe in the recesses of all men's hearts this too is
    their desire.

This is the peace which passes all understanding.
This is your peace.

A man begins to kick out at the world but ends up kicking
    himself because the key to all his fears and troubles
    begins and ends in himself.
Where you are there is great peace. Without you there is
    discord.

I know that in your time you answer all prayers, and I
    leave all my troubles and fears on your doorstep.

Thank you for today, Father,
for a good service and for fellowship.

I pray for all my friends and Christians everywhere.
Fill our hearts with your love, good Lord.
Strengthen our faith and protect our way.
This we ask through our Lord Jesus Christ.

Hope

I was asked today if I had ever been angry at you. We both know that I have but that was between ourselves and mostly by evening my anger had subsided, to be replaced by fresh hope, plus the assurance that whatever had happened was most surely for my own ultimate good.

At night I thanked you for your insight into my affairs.

Lord, my hope tonight is for my friends, that they may all come to know you better, and that you will reveal yourself to them and become their personal saviour. Also, that the men in this prison may come to know you, if not right away, then in time.

Teach me to witness for you quietly and sincerely and I pray that you forgive any that have done me any kind of wrong and that I too may forgive them, despite any ill will between us.

I also pray that you forgive me for any that have received harm from my hands or tongue, and let your peace come, as a soothing balm, to troubled minds and spirits.

Doubting Thomas

Tonight I felt compelled to go and talk with a man.
Don't ask me why. I don't know.

We spoke of so many things,
and for the first time we both crossed a barrier of doubt,
and saw each other as we really are.

It is a strange thing that two of my best hours in this
    prison should be spent in his company.
What makes it strange, Lord, is that the central topic of
    our conversation was you.
What makes it even stranger is that this man does not
    profess to be a Christian.

His name is Thomas.

His life has not been easy, and he is desperately searching
for his destiny, but, like the Thomas of old, the roots of
doubt need to be pulled firmly out of his life, so that he
can breathe a fresher air than he ever thought possible.

It is with a profound sense of shock in talking in Thomas
that I saw the doubting Thomas in us all.

It is we who imprison Christ daily with our doubt,
and in our moments of need we shout over the wall.

'Jesus, are you there?'
'Jesus, can you hear me?'
Silence.

'Look, Jesus, I know you're there. I need your help. I'm
    sorry for doubting you.'
'Look, here is a small bundle of belief.'
A small bundle is seen going over the wall.
Jesus picks up the bundle and knocks on the door.
Thomas opens the door very slightly.

Thomas: Err, look, can I 'ave a look at your
                wounds, mate?

Nothing.

Thomas: Well, look, it's a bit on the late side and
                it's getting dark and I'm too tired to hang
                about. Maybe you can come back when
                it's light and I can see a bit better.

So, Jesus settles down in a new prison of doubt erected
by Thomas. He waits and waits but no more bundles get
thrown over the wall. Meanwhile, Thomas has opened
the door, but as he lets nothing go through it, nothing
comes out.

   Father, for all the doubting Thomases in the world,
break down the walls, and let us trust you. Let us trust
you with a child's trust in his father.

Blessings

Father, sitting here in my cell, I am thinking of all the people at this moment praying to you.
Your multicoloured, multinational children,
praying for anything and everything.
How many people are praying for me, I wonder?
People I don't know, people I've never met, people under great strain and in sadness.
How many of those noble people pray for the men and women behind walls tonight?
I don't really feel lonesome, Lord. In fact I feel quite good.
Contentment seals my life.
I've got a lot of friends, Lord, and a lot of folk who really do care.
Please accept my prayers tonight for all these good people.
may you truly bless them with your peace and trust.

Prayer

I feel great sadness, Lord,
when I realise how selfish I have been in the past,
so engulfed in my own self-pity that I failed to comprehend
the goodness and friendship that was within arm's reach.
Blindness, Lord, is a terrible thing – and there are none
so blind as those who will not see.
My prayers, Father, have indeed opened my eyes.

Tonight I pray for the spiritually blind.
I pray you will open their eyes, as you have mine.
I pray for the souls of all people in prison.
I pray for those behind locked doors of their own
making.
I pray for those alone and frightened.
I pray for those without the ability or the knowledge to
pray to you for themselves.

Give them peace of mind, Lord.

I pray for all people who are social outcasts and misfits.
I pray for families of prisoners and others who are
separated by walls or time or distance.

The Freedom to Come

Lord,

what are the years to you
but an atom of time?

Tomorrow?
What of tomorrow?
For you, Lord, are truly the promise of tomorrow.

In your timelessness, your limitlessness,
you are eternity.
That truly is our tomorrow:
>   no pain,
>   no fear,
>   no worry,
>   no sickness,
>   no war internal or external,
>   no sorrowful days,
>   no nights of doubt,
For in your love, Lord Jesus, all is truly bright light.

Man's time is hard time.
Where you are, Lord, there is no time but the present,
through which your eternal presence
fills and is everything.

>   Maranatha.
>   Our Lord Jesus come.

Cross-eyed People

Father, you love each and every one of us most dearly,
    for you have told us so, and you sent your Son to
    die on the cross.

So, perhaps 'Cross-eyed' people are the richest.

What else can a man say in the light of such overwhelming
    evidence of love but,
'Father, my God, I thank you for making me Cross-eyed
    and taking away the most extreme poverty of all,
that of not knowing you.
All you have is mine.
All you ask is that I believe.
When one has nothing – belief is but a small price to
    pay.
I believe.'

Lord,
I thank you for a fine peaceful day,
for a good service, and a true sermon,
for good fellowship and kindly words.

I pray for peace in the world.
I pray for peace in myself.
I pray for peace in the lives and hearts of my family and
    friends.

In Your Peace

Only yesterday someone told me that I had gained a pearl at a great price.

This treasure cost me thirteen years of my life spent in prison, and only you know how many more.

Father, teach me how to use the years that only good may come and please let me be responsible enough not to put myself at risk, or abuse my time.

You have given me many things in your time – pain, distress, anger, worry, fear, mistrust – all these things have been my teachers. You taught me well. For my own good you schooled me for life and at a very deep level. For I laboured in the darkness of Solomon's mines, and came up and out with the true gold of life.

I humbly thank you. For the times I doubted you, for the times I rejected, and the times I objected – forgive me, Lord. I am a misguided sinner.

Lord, you came into this world to call sinners, bringing back all those who stand at a distance from you.

We cannot love two masters. Teach us to set our hearts on your treasure, and to live in your peace eternally.

Christmas

People of different faiths share the love, peace and brotherhood of Christ as we celebrate his birthday.

I have seen you, Lord, shining out of people as they greet each other with friendly smiles and sincere good wishes.

There have been times when I've sat in hell and prayed and prayed for just a glimmer of the festive season.

Once it came in the form of a drunk, three floors above me in his cell, singing 'Away in a manger' and 'We three kings of Orient are'. At 11.30 p.m. on Christmas Eve he couldn't sing in tune and he was undoubtedly annoying some of the other prisoners in Wandsworth.

To me, sitting in silence in my cell, it was like a heavenly choir of angels. He made me laugh for the first time in days when, on the stroke of midnight, he shouted at the top of his voice, 'Gentlemen and fellow prisoners, I bid you all a merry and happy Christmas.'

I do not believe people understand just how much it means when you are in prison and you, Lord Jesus, light up the world with your great love.

We share this wonderful day, the biggest birthday party the world has ever known. We might be outside it all, looking in, as it were, but you, Jesus, are right there with us, saying, 'Happy birthday, Chris.'

'You too, my Lord.'

Goodnight, Lord

Father, thank you for today.

For the people I have been able to meet,
for the little good I have been able to do.

For my work, which while hard was both good and
beneficial.
For the sunshine and fresh air,
for trust, faith, hope and love.

Thank you for friends and loved ones.

May your grace and peace be on them and on all
mankind.

Grant me a peaceful night of rest
and grant it to the world.

Goodnight, Lord.

Friend

Truly you are indeed gift.
All I can give you in return is the friendship which you
   give me.
Were my heart an oaken chest, you would open it
   and see
all that belongs to me, belongs to thee.

Watch over Me

Help me to say 'Yes' to the demands you make of me, because in my weakness I am still a man of little worth, who without your support could do no good thing.

Lord, this night I am completely in your hands. Do with me as you will. Help me to know your will for me so that through me some good may come to your name.

Father, this night I pray for all men who sit in prisons of darkness living in fear of what the future holds for them; for those who suffer from frustration, apathy; for those who have lost faith and for those who seek you for the first time.

Please be within reach of all of them, and in your mercy grant them peace.

Thank you for my work, which I now offer back to you.

Thank you for the people, whoever they may be, who made my day a little easier to bear.

Thank you for friends, for hope, for insight into your will for me.

May the world be at peace and rest.

May I be at peace and rest.

May you watch over me this night.

Good Deed

Hugh, our chaplain, will be leaving us shortly and, because I wanted him to have something different by which he could remember us, I set about getting him a card, which hopefully both he and his family would keep and treasure as a gift from the people here in Coldingly, in recognition of all the good he has done during his stay.

Somehow things don't always work out the way we expect, because our good deed might thwart someone else's good deed and thereby cause distress or pain.

The card which I made came from the back cover of a *Reader's Digest*, together with a piece of hardboard and the goodwill of Mick, a fellow prisoner who painted a design and the words which I thought might be appropriate.

But another man had gone to the trouble to buy a card and truly meant well by it. He may have been a little hurt by being upstaged, so I ask in sincerity that a solution may come, whereby no hurt will come out of two worthwhile good deeds.

It can hardly matter who takes the credit, if any, as long as the good deed has been done.

Instrument of Peace

Father, I do earnestly and sincerely pray for all who are in any way persecuted and victimised this day. Please give them the strength and courage to face their trials. May you send them the Comforter to comfort them in all their distress and rejection and may only good come out of their affliction.

Lord, let us, like St Francis, be instruments of your peace. If I cannot speak good, let me say nothing, and keep my tongue from evil. But let me not flinch from any duty which calls me to do right.

I would pray for all prisoners this night, because we have to live daily with so much ignorance, so much false pride, so much hate, so much mistrust, so much fear, all concentrated within a small area of this greatly troubled earth.

Lord, only you have the power to dispel such a cloud of darkness which blights so many lives. In this year please work a miracle in our prisons.

Strength in Weakness

Lord,

Take these hands
and teach me to use them in your name.

These eyes, Lord, take them and use them
so that I can see all that is worthy:

Merit,
     trust,
          truth,
               peace,
                    love,
                         goodness,
                         faith,
                         hope,
                         strength,
                         mercy,
                         compassion.

Let me see through the glass clearly.

These lips and this tongue,
let them praise you all the days of my life.
Praise and speak of what is right,
give me the words so that I never
profane your righteousness.

Give me a heart like yours with
the strength to love, despite all human folly.

Give me the will to do what is right,
not in my might but in my trust in you,
for your strength is made perfect

in my weakness.

40

The Right Track?

Perhaps somehow I am on the wrong track in my conversations with people. We talk about this and that, but somehow we seem to be on different levels. They have their here and now, where they can see, feel and touch things which are important to them.

The things which are important to me belong in some hopefully not-too-distant time and place.

The children's stories which you have given me the gift of being able to write cause me unspeakable embarrassment. I wonder why this should be so, when they have been a source of pleasure to some people. Not a few of them are children who have had a parent missing from their lives owing to imprisonment. Perhaps that is why I have felt this gift is also a responsibility.

I have just seen an old person on the television speaking of her faith. The thing which impressed me the most was the fact that she had for seventy-eight years gone through a troubled world, seen much distress, lost many loved ones and good friends. Yet still she kept her faith.

Lord, I pray that I too should never lose my faith in you and have to wander in some spiritual wilderness.

Lord, during my times of stress and trial, be ever near me. Lord, enable me to go on and forward in the spirit of peace and contentment. Grant me the composure and strength of mind and soul to see the good in people.

And in this place, such as it is, let me be aware that I am not the only one who has to endure humiliation and degradation. and if it be your will, give me the strength to help others to know you.

My Friend

Father, tonight I would like to speak to you about my friend. He is old now, and I don't see him as often as I once did, and I miss him.

Sitting here in the quiet of my cell, I look up at the overcast sky and I can see his face. In trying to describe him to you the words don't come as easily as I thought but, Lord, it won't be too long, 'at his age', before he joins you, and your gain is going to be my greatest loss.

I think about all the lonely railway stations where he shared a word of comfort and a cup of tea with the wives and girlfriends of the men in our prison. I remember the young children who he bought a bit of food for, out of his pension, and how they would flock round our table on a visiting day.

If you were to say to him, 'Come into my kingdom because you have deserved it', he would not be able to understand you. For he is blind to the world, and already lives in your kingdom.

Father, I offer you my friend. Please take care of him. Give him your love. Help him to come to know you better, and grant him the peace, health and happiness his life merits.

42

In Your Name

Take my mind and think through it,
cleanse it daily of all pollution.
Let your cleansing peace flow through it
until I am one with you.

Take my mind and think through it
beyond earthbound creation to divine infinity,
to be overwhelmed by your cataclysm of love,
to soar to the swirling heavens of reverential joy,
to make my consciousness cry out:
        'Spiritum, Sanctum, Dominum et vivicantem'.

Take my brain,
give me right and true discernment, wisdom and justice,
so that I may think more clearly, and be precise.

Take these feet and lead them on a road
to the heart of the Christian message.
In your name never let them wander
lest they stumble and fall, and if they should,
Jesus, pick me up and lead me on.

This Garden Planet

My job in prison, Father, is tending the gardens. It is a job I care about, because you have opened my eyes and taught me to care. Often I work hard with only your help and guidance to fire me. Father, when I look back on a piece of ground on which I have laboured, over which I have prayed, it is a very rewarding and gratifying experience.

The trouble is that when I leave that piece of work and go on to something else, I leave with a heavy heart, knowing that my fellow prisoners will abuse it by throwing their waste out of the windows, harming the earth.

There's nothing personal in it. They just don't think, and moreover, they don't seem to care.

The scattered bits of rubbish all over the gardens and in the flower-beds reminds me of how we have treated this garden planet you have given us.

Now, Father, like you, I care.

I care enough to keep the good things out of harm's way.

Blossoming

As I go about my daily labour in the prison gardens, it is with eyes of wonder that I am able to see your invisible hand helping me out in all that I touch and do, and even when my day's toil is over, your work continues. Tenderly touching, caressing, tending every bit of soil, each bulb, plant, root and branch in this, your world.

I pass a tree and see bare branches. And later I pass the tree again. It is with unfailing awed wonder that I see the branches bearing leaves and buds. Then later still when I pass the tree, I behold the spectacle of life in full blossom and colour.

Lord, Father, work with us and in us, through us and around us.

It is in this knowledge that I feel both a sense of responsibility to you and myself, so much so that I try to put as much of myself into my work as is possible and work alongside you, the one truly trusted and tried. Losing all sense of time and place, except for the here and now, where all that counts is the task at hand.

I don't profess in any way to be a gardener, for beside you who can be a gardener? But, Father, you know I work hard and I feel very privileged to be your labourer.

Thank You, Lord

Father, tonight I am happy because I can smell the freshness of the garden driving away the stale prison stench which engulfs and permeates this place.

Thank you for helping me complete another college paper and, despite everything, for allowing me to remain basically simple – which is a rare gift in itself.

We've come a long way, haven't we, Father? It's never been easy. Yet somehow more and more I believe in my heart that we shall transcend the ties of this world and enter the world where we will receive a just reward for our labours.

I spent some time with a few nice people, who helped to make the day a little easier. Help me to see more good people and to be a positive help to others.

Fathers, tonight I pray for all the warring nations and other factions in the world where innocent people live in fear and terror, suffering death and injustice as their daily lot.

Help us all to see that we have a cross to bear, and may we lift it with a good will, and carry it rather than pull it along with resentment.

Thank you, Lord, for today.

Please give my family and friends your love and your perfect peace.

Dove of Peace

On waking this morning, before the doors were unlocked, I noticed a small shape nestling on my bed, and to my great surprise I saw it was a snow-white dove. About half a dozen fly about the prison quite freely, and one had come in, I imagine, for shelter and rest. When I looked up to the window, I noticed another one sitting on top of my writing-desk.

I just lay in my bed meditating on this symbol of peace.

When the door was opened with a loud noise the pair flew back out of the window. But it was, nonetheless, a good start to the day.

After breakfast I went off to work. The sun was blazing down, bringing a smile to the lips, and a feeling of good companionship filled the air.

Before my work I went off to cut some roses for the chapel. After I had cut a good bunch I went off to start my work and I picked up my tools and set about it with a will. I am clearing a piece of ground so that it can be turned into a garden, Lord. I truly hope justice can be done to it in your name. Where there is now rubble you and I together will create a garden where beautiful things may some day grow, if it be your will.

Roses

Father, today while I was working in the garden, I came upon the most beautiful red rose. Its fragrance I could not describe. It transported me to a world where there was nothing but your truth and goodness.

Unbeknown to me, some people were observing my actions as I cupped the fullness of the rose in both hands and sniffed at its centre. As I walked away one man commented, 'It's beautiful, isn't it? You're a lucky man.' Yes, perhaps I am lucky, but the far greater truth which I have learned is that man, with all his modern microchip technology, cannot create the beauty and fullness of a rose.

For it comes from you, goes back to you, and each year is reborn to a new life in you.

What have we to compare with such beauty and perfection?

In truth, Lord of creation, we your human race have nothing if we have not you to create even each tiny second for us. How much more must we owe you for all the other good things which you give us? And yet we give you back so little. You bear with us. Your great patience never runs out. Your tolerance towards us is ever constant. Your strength renews man so that he can raise himself above all the tragedies and pain of this mortal life, and your great love gives us the roses.

Help Me, Father

Lord, I'm not really complaining but you see, there's a lot of earth and bricks, stones and dead weeds at the back of the fence near 'B' wing, behind the rose bed, and I haven't got a shovel to move it. (The one I had broke off at the handle and no one will replace it.) So I've been using a dustpan which people somehow think is rather quaint.

I could say, 'It doesn't matter', but you see you've always treated me right and if I don't finish the job, it's like cheating.

Why Wait?

The apples are ripe.
The tree waits
See the golden boughs
weighted down with the fruit
of delight and love.
Golden delicious.
Reach out and touch,
taste and see, they are good
God-given gifts
from on high, for me.

Who would take and share?
For as the tree cannot withhold the fruit,
neither can we, my friend,
for we all have a duty to share.
What we have been given is given in love.

To Forgive Each Other

I turn a shovelful of rich dark earth
and see a cosmos of life, within arm's reach.
I feel the essence of your Spirit in everything.
The wind brushes through the trees,
the leaves rustle with joy at the touch of your breath.
The flowers smile when the sun shines on them
and cry when you send the rain.

To see a rose on a rainy day
is akin to seeing both you and your despair over us,
your frail human beings.

Father, only you are truly good.

Thank you for today.
Please bless my family and friends.
Forgive those who have hurt me in any way,
and grant me the goodwill and strength to forgive them.
And if not right away, then in time. May we forgive
     each other.

Dad

Today I went to see my father – he is dying. Today I sat beside him and for the first time ever, I spoke the truth of my heart to his heart. My words were:

Dad, my father, I've never said these words to any man but you're the only man I've ever really respected in my whole life. Sometimes a man cries for the pain and loss in his heart.

Dad, my father, I want you to know I love you with all my heart and may that love give you renewed strength. My friend, my dad, my father, I am truly sorry. Sorry for all the pain that I have ever caused you and at the loss of all the wisdom which you ever tried to give me.

I thank you for always being near me in my hours of desperate need and trial. If I was ever ungrateful, as I most surely was, many times, I pray for your forgiveness. You were the bravest, kindest man I ever knew. Yours was the true gold on the counter of my life.

Tonight I feel sickened. I am tired. I feel ugly and dirty. I feel crushed. I feel a thousand years old behind my daily mask of hope and patience. I am revolted by what I have let my life make of all my good dreams, of which you were a part. Rest easy, my friend of infinite goodness.

Lord, I ask that you help me to carry this burden of infinite sadness. Help me to bear the weight of grief and loss, and help me to work for a closer unity with you, and may I someday share your profound joy in life again.

They Don't Understand

Father, how I wish that I could touch all our yesterdays, today. I would go back to childhood and sit at the feet of my earthly father, as he spoke the wisdom of his heart which came from you. I wish I could look into his eyes of goodness and love and see and share his dreams for me, the future he planned. He had it all so clear in his mind's eye with any number of alternatives should one plan go wrong. Yes, but they were all meant to carry a burden of hard work!

His way was a good example and he knew I was capable – of what? I didn't know myself. Yes, I see it all now so clearly. My wild, reckless, uncaring youth. My God, I knew it all! Today, Lord, I know nothing!

Could I but walk the heath with him, as in days of old, or meet him at Regent's Park, or watch him with his friends. If I could see him smile and laugh and speak in his native tongue, hear him admonish me for some wrong act, hear his determined, resolute tread as he walked a hard road, look into his eyes after he had suffered some prejudice or discrimination. They would be calm and quiet and his answer to my words of rage, 'Dad, why?' would be one of understanding – 'Ignorance and misunderstanding, boy, and senseless hatred against what they don't understand.'

The Gold of My Life

Father, today I was told that my dad's condition had deteriorated with pneumonia and that he had slipped into a coma. I sit here in a cell shaking my head, trying not to let any morbid thoughts get a grip on my mind. There is no one with whom I can talk.

Can a fellow prisoner offer anything but a quiet embarrassed word of solace and comfort to soften the blow? A screw barks out his inhumanity for he leaves his feelings and compassion and torch of human decency at home. Every day he leaves to join in the daily din, as the day lifts the lid on society's human meat factories and dustbins.

Lord, tonight I am hungry. Dad could cook food that would make every angel in heaven come back for seconds! I believe that you too, Father, might, like Oliver, come back for more. Beam him up, Lord; don't let him suffer, please.

Dad, you said, 'Don't cry!' Sometimes, my friend, it's hard. Sure, my tears are selfish because my love for you is selfish! It was special! It was good! It was decent! Now, like so much of me, I can't express it in words any more. That's what these tears are for, Dad. I want to scream out the rage of my heart up into the midnight sky.

Do not go quietly or gently into that good night. Get the spirit of fire and live! We love and need you.

Jesus, you've got my best friend. Take care of him – the gold of my life.

Into your hands I commend his spirit.

Immeasurable Loss

People who are trying to be kind and ease the pain of immeasurable loss tell me he was old. Does love ever grow old? You, Lord, are two thousand years old. Has your love ever grown old or cold? No, my friend, it hasn't, and it never will. The golden tears of my heart tell me the love I have for my father, and the love he had for me, his prodigal son, can never ever grow old or cold.

It was my privilege both to have known this man and to have observed him as a member of your human race. From my vantage point I saw him leave it a lot better for his illuminating presence. What am I going to say now?

Pain? Yes! Hurt? Yes! Loss!

Yes, bereft!

Yes, grief!

Yes, sadness!

Yes, robbed!

Yes, emptiness!

Yes, numb!

The circle of despair – almost. Robbed of his presence? Yes, just for the time being, but in the Spirit, never! Lord, you asked your apostles could they not watch one hour with you. Were they asleep or had the heaviness, which is placed on the heart through human tragedy, closed their eyes?

My father of the immeasurable overflowing heart, your work is now done. Like our Blessed Lord, you have left your daily cross and come to your immortal rest.

Sleep on, brave one. Day is done; rest in peace; you have surely earned it.

Lazarus Tip

Dear God, all-merciful Father,

Here at the tip it's peaceful and quiet. The skies are blue and it's not too cold, looking out over the fields which have been prepared for next year's harvest. I can see the beautiful greens and yellows on the trees.

A hawk hangs suspended in mid-air, awaiting its prey. Nature is both cruel and kind – on the one hand showing me its beauty, and the hawk its food – yet we are both bonded by the fact that we live off the land which provides us with sustenance.

There are quite a number of us occupying the tip: white-tailed rabbits, stoats, crows, field mice, hares, foxes, partridges, pheasants, magpies, herons, wrens, finches, the odd adder, frogs and fish which are down in the freshwater stream called Gallows Brook, and we all exist like a proper family, not interfering in each other's business.

I am grateful for my job, Lord. It wouldn't be everyone's cup of tea, because it's in the middle of nowhere: no main roads, no shops, just a long winding lane, with the odd farmhouse in the distance. People say, 'Don't you get lonely, or bored, or fed up?'

Lord Jesus, I have you as my constant companion. You are here with me right now. In you I always have a friend who I can talk to and if no one can understand my secret of life in the tip, I know you do. You brought me to this place in the wilderness, named after your friend Lazarus who you raised to life from the grave, just as you raise me from the pit. You have always known my deeper needs, and while I was praying you were acting for good on my behalf. Being human and frail, I have worries, fears

56

and doubts, but where there is confusion and turmoil you bring colour and peace.

Into your hands I place Caroline and the infant in her womb, my darlings Christopher and Holly, my whole life and our home.

Ever gratefully yours, Jesus.

Mum

I don't know why you had to send so much rain but no doubt you have your reasons. The rain makes me think of a time early after my mother died. My little niece, Karen, was looking out of the window at the downpour and said, 'Nanna is doing her washing.'

Mum's been gone a long time now, twenty years or more. Karen is a grown woman. How time flies.

Mum's memory hasn't faded one bit. I can still see her going off for the first real holiday in her life, a comparatively young woman of forty-eight and just never coming back. I often think of the void she left behind, which was never ever filled, the grief, the sadness, the pain, what should have been, what might have been.

How could I believe in you, Lord? I didn't. I thought that if you were true, I hated you for taking the light out of my life and that you were cruel, unkind, unfair. I raged against you.

Yet it was perhaps my mother's prayers which helped me to believe in you. Now I can look into my children's eyes and see her soul. Children's china blue eyes, just like hers. Holly's smile, just like hers.

I feel very peaceful in Holly's presence now, just as I do in yours. Praise you, Lord Jesus. Please take care of Holly, Christopher and Caroline and the new life which she holds in her womb. The sun is shining, Father, and its warm tender rays embrace me.

Letter to Angie

Sometimes, once a lifetime, you perhaps feel there is someone who you have wanted to reach out to, but you have to think of that person's ability to cope with your intrusion into their life.

In my case it was my young daughter. The last time I saw her she was just eighteen months old, crawling across the floor to me, stumbling to get the words 'Da da' to form.

Now she's a woman, and I am some shadow from way back out of sight, and out of mind. Yet time, distance and experience can never erase the paternal feelings I have for my daughter, and in the stillness of my heart I will always treasure the memory of that little part of me which is walking in this world, living and breathing, laughing and crying and trying to cope with her world as she sees it.

There may well be many people who have the same feelings and longings which I carry with me through my life. If there are, I wish them the peace which fills the mind with good things and the ability to hope that even better things might perhaps come their way in the journey through the future.

A Father's Prayer

Lord, I have been reading about a small girl who has fallen down a disused well. She is only eighteen months old and rescue workers are trying to reach her. She has been down the well for more than thirty hours. People are praying round the hole for her recovery and well-being. I add my prayers to theirs for her safety.

In praying for this child, I can't help visualising my own children, two lovely little people, just fourteen months old. Holly: demanding, bouncy, strong and fearless, and sometimes quite kind. Christopher, her twin brother: gentle, kind, firm, and sturdy, a very nice little person, full of life and energy.

Caroline and I both realise that we are only a part of their life. At times you can see their security lies not in us but in each other. They chatter away to each other in a language all their own. They share the vision and wonder of each new day with one another. They are happy and secure in each other's attention and love.

Jesus, I praise and thank you for my two little people. Just to have one child used to be a most precious and cherished dream but, in giving us two, you have enriched our lives immensely. Life is never empty. Innocent love surrounds us, and never a day goes by without our home being enriched by laughter and joy.

For my part love has never really been fulfilled. I hold my children in my arms after a long day's work and feel their pure simple love embrace me . Make me a good and kind father, just as you are. You give me patience and understanding, wisdom and tolerance, strength and compassion that I may be deserving of the love you have bestowed on my heart and in my life.

Make me appreciate all the good you bring into my life. Let not the cares of the world grind me down to a point where I cannot see your goodness everywhere in everything. Thank you, Father, for Holly and Christopher and may you love, guide and protect them always.

With love from father to Father.

October 1987

Another wet and windy day down on the land. Dark clouds all around. My toes are so cold, they feel numb. But there are moments of beauty as I watch the trees dance to the song of the wind, swaying and swirling with each gust blowing full force.

The man on the radio reported gales up to a hundred miles per hour, floods and devastation, people being made homeless, ships capsizing, death and destruction. There are and will be many who will need your loving hand to uplift heavy hearts this day, I am sad to say.

I pray most earnestly that all will be comforted by your presence in their lives. Thank you, Jesus, for keeping our family safe and warm.

Life is not easy at this time with another baby on the way, On the one hand there are trials and tribulations, on the other there is the knowledge that as we face each one, we grow closer to you and stronger. We are fortunate in that you have provided me with a job, a nice home, and a beautiful young family, food on our table, self-respect and dignity. Yet I can still remember the days of despair when I had none of these things and apathy was a constant companion.

If at times, Lord, I don't appear grateful and I don't stop and say thank you for everything, please forgive me. Life moves so very fast from minute to minute, hour to hour, day to day. You know in my heart I always find myself on the road leading back to my home in you.

I pray that you will reveal yourself to Caroline, just as you have revealed yourself to me. I know she loves you as I do, yet she sometimes gets wrapped up in the cares of this world and it's hard to reach her when this happens. Open her heart more fully, Jesus, and pour in the new wine of your Spirit so that she may be what you would have her be in your most precious love.

Rain

Father, Lord almighty,

It has rained all day, and the water is squelching round my toes inside my wellington boots, and running from my hair down inside my shirt. Very uncomfortable indeed. Only another couple of hours and then I can go home to the warmth of my family, and a nice cup of tea.

I hope Caroline is all right. It's only a couple of days now until the baby is due. This morning we thought it was on its way, and we got prepared to leave for the hospital, and then our little crisis passed. Caroline felt a little better. About five thirty Holly and Christopher woke. I heated milk and fed them. Then quietness fell over the house once again.

Sometimes it's hard to tear myself away from those I love but I know you are looking after them while I go out to earn our daily bread and help keep a roof over our heads.

It's a source of strength knowing you are near because there are days when I could quite easily say that I've had enough of rain and mud, feeling filthy, uncomfortable, lonely and bored. It's then a still small voice speaks softly in my ear: 'Come unto me all ye that labour and are weary. Learn of me, for my yoke is easy and my burden is light. I am the life, the truth and the way.'

The Prayer of a Redundant Man

Lord Jesus,

You have always been with me through the good and bad times in my life and I have much to thank you for. Yet now – dispirited, hurt and rejected – I can feel the clammy hand of apathy bending my head in shame as I look upon my children three, and my wife with a heart of gold.

All I can do is sigh, perplexed about tomorrow, yet frightened by today.

Bills pile up, house in jeopardy, children's future in ruins, plans gone astray.

I go from job centre to agency – 'Sorry, no jobs today'.

What shall I do, Lord? You alone know.

The sun shines brightly and the wind blows cold.

Night falls and there is only you who understand me as I understand you.

I am close to tears that seem to be in vain.

People come and go,

money in their pockets their fields to sow.

Lord, I don't want too much from life:

just to see my children grow.

What is wrong and what is right?

I don't feel I can give up the fight.

There is something for me, for us, for everyone, Lord, my prayer is that it comes sooner rather than later. Would I commit a crime? Yes, maybe, but not against you, Lord, and not against my family.

Jesus and St Jude help this redundant man to win the war.

Chris.

Never Stop Loving

I saw a couple who were maybe sixty-five, hiking along the road, holding hands. I had to stop and tell them how moved I was, because in my own life that was all I ever wanted, just to hold hands with my wife. I told them I was going through a painful break-up. The lady reached into the car and held my hand. The man said it takes two people wanting the same thing. No matter how good you are, you cannot do it alone. His words did give me some perspective and insight, but no relief.

Later I went to see Bill and Pearl, kind and thoughtful Christian friends. I told them about the way things were and the difficulty to be faced. They listened sympathetically and with maturity. Both said, 'Chris, time heals.' I wondered about people dying, about broken hearts. Could it be true? There was I in the eye of the storm, and I didn't really believe that I would ever get well again. They prayed that I might be given peace, and that Caroline would feel she wasn't so alone. How does one cope? In looking to Jesus is the answer. Never stop loving. Never stop caring.

Distant Things

It's two in the morning and sleep just won't come. Away in the distance I can hear the sound of tyres on a motorway. Somewhere to go, going somewhere. For the time being I have nowhere to go, going nowhere, life in the cotton wool. Lights in the distance batter and beckon me. God, grant me the serenity to accept the things I cannot change, the courage to change the things I can and the wisdom to know the difference. I want to change my wife. I want to take away her hurt, her pain, her deception. Because these are *her* desires that are catching hold of me. If I pray, I think she will get better, but that's not reality. My reality is nothing in the room and wondering if this weight I carry will ever be lifted by unseen hands. Expectations and hope arise.

Regrets

Here on my bed I lie, having somehow got through the day. At about five thirty last evening a bailiff came to the door to serve a further warrant on me from my wife and the mother of my children so that I can be dragged off to a prison cell. Having taken everything, she now wants the free air I breathe. Where did my wife go? The woman with whom I had five babes? Holding hands and pushing through, sharing the joys of life and love, there is my wife – the one who was sick and had to be nursed, the one who didn't want any fuss. Where is my wife who pushed me away in her ups and downs? Where is the caring mother of five with the strength and joy to overcome adversity?

Where is the love of my life, my pride and joy? Oh, tell me it was just my imagination playing tricks with fantasy and she didn't really exist. But she was my lady and my wife. She wasn't fantasy. She was the most real thing that ever happened in my wretched life. She picked me up when I was down. She brought me warmth and caring touch. But she didn't know I cared, and that's my fault.

The Early Morning Rain

Woke at seven thirty. Another long night, only three hours' sleep. Fighting off the options, looking at reasons and feeling so frightened and alone. Wanting, no needing to be the guilty one. Then playing at accuser. Red boiling molten blood coursing through veins of rage, animal-like in my cage, I lick my real and imaginary wounds. Outside it's cold and damp and already I feel the chill of night coming in.

I'm all right now for a moment between the tears. Like a child, I want and need somebody's hand to hold, to tell me it will soon get better. I can find a million reasons for resurrecting the love we had, but perhaps the truth is that my wife has no love.

Crying eyes never lie. They just feel the pain.

Lady of Charity

When you are feeling as if down is never going to end, just leave doors and windows open, and sure as a hot day in hell, something good is bound to happen. I seemed to be in control when I woke this morning, as though a great weight had been lifted. Yet I still felt fairly numb and battered. As such things need to be done, I went to see a solicitor.

Afterwards I went to a charity shop. I picked up some things, and went towards a changing room. While I was waiting, the curtain was opened by a lady wearing a blue spotted dress. She turned and looked at me for approval. I said she looked stunning, and probably could go anywhere wearing such a dress. She said she had no one to take her; she then went back into the changing room, and came out with something else on, which didn't suit her. She asked my opinion and I gave it. She looked at me, smiled and said, 'I suppose not.' I felt warmth and appreciation and as if I was special enough to have an opinion. And the pirouette in the changing room was a theatre for a full house of one, for which I will be ever grateful.

We may never meet again, lady of charity, but I thank you.

Dreams of Yesterday

They say tomorrow never comes
but we have today 1,440 minutes
which, if they were pounds, would make us
very rich.

So why not spend them wisely and well?
Building something which will make
your dreams of yesterday something to remember,
fun-loving and healthy,
that makes tomorrow worth its weight in gold.

Footfalls in Memory

Reflections from Solitude

Terry Waite

For the first year of Terry Waite's solitary confinement in Beirut he was given nothing to read. During those days not only did he write his autobiography in his head, but he also attempted to remember the books, poems and prayers he had read during his life. Eventually his guards mellowed and he was given books.

Now Terry Waite has collected together a selection from the books he remembered, the books he received and the books he wished he had been given. This selection evokes images of childhood, travels and captivity as he vividly recalls personal stories and anecdotes and as he takes the reader down the corridors of his memory.

This captivating anthology . . . makes an unusually impressive prison book to add to that genre

Ronald Blyth, *Church Times*

From this anthology flows a strange sense of how terrible and how wonderful to have your guard appearing holding something book-shaped in his hand and the injunction to "read slow"

Libby Purves, *The Times*

ISBN 0 340 66922 5

The Street Children of Brazil

One Woman's Remarkable Story

Sarah de Carvalho

From the world of television to the streets of Brazil

Her glittering career in film production and TV production took her to California, Sydney and London. But her international lifestyle and fast-lane salary gave her no time to enjoy herself.

Through a series of remarkable events, Sarah left her career and joined a missionary organisation in Brazil. There she met children from the age of seven living on the streets, taking drugs, stealing to survive and open to prostitution and gang warfare.

This is the remarkable true story of a life transformed. It tells of the incredible work that Sarah de Carvalho and her husband have founded in the Happy Child Mission. It is a story of immense faith, suffering and love. The children whose stories are revealed in this exceptional book will change the heart of every reader.

ISBN 0 340 64164 9

The Colour of Darkness

A Personal Story of Tragedy and Hope in Rwanda

Lesley Bilinda

Tear Fund health worker Lesley Bilinda was on leave when the killing began. Her husband, Rwandan pastor Charles Bilinda, had stayed behind. She never heard from him again.

Months of agony and uncertainty followed. Lesley could only pray. Where was Charles? What had happened to the beautiful country she loved so much?

Returning to Rwanda, she was rocked to the core: homes destroyed, whole families wiped out, tremendous suffering in crowded refugee camps, the pain on her friends' faces. But in the midst of this darkness and her own tragedy, Lesley also found light and hope: miraculous escapes from certain death, kindness and courage in the face of violent hatred, and above all faith in God.

An inspiration to all those who share in the ministry of Tear Fund.

David Adeney

This heart-rending story is a simple testimony to a God who loves us through our worst nightmares. It is guaranteed to rekindle faith and hope in all those who wonder where God has gone.

Clive Calver, Director General, Evangelical Alliance

Lesley Bilinda is now Assistant to Tear Fund's Scottish Coordinator, and runs the Charles Bilinda Memorial Trust.

ISBN 0 340 64279 3

Miracles Can Happen

True Stories of Divine Encounter

Phil Shirley

Do you believe in miracles?

A child is healed of a life-threatening illness, an accident is narrowly avoided, a woman defies medical experts and walks again. For those who witnessed them, these are divine miracles.

Miracles Can Happen brings together thirty of the most remarkable stories from around the world including the experiences of Corrie ten Boom and Brother Andrew. For both the sceptical and those already convinced, each fascinating tale touches the heart and challenges the mnd.

Open the book – join the debate

Phil Shirley is a professional writer and regular contributor to several national newspapers and magazines.

ISBN 0 340 65625 5